PENGUIN BOOKS

TALES FROM HERODOTUS

Herodotus, who lived in the fifth century BC, is thought to have travelled widely throughout Egypt, Africa, and many Greek city-states. Written with wit and vitality, his *Histories* embrace all aspects of life, from war and betrayal to ancient landmarks, customs and tales of the animal kingdom.

Herdotus is acknowledged as the first great historian.

The complete edition of *The Histories* by Herodotus is published in Penguin Classics.

D1494384

TALES FROM
HERODOTUS

TRANSLATED BY
AUBREY DE SÉLINCOURT

PENGUIN BOOKS

PENGUIN BOOKS

Published by the Penguin Group
Penguin Books Ltd, 27 Wrights Lane, London w8 5TZ
Penguin Books USA Inc., 375 Hudson Street, New York, New York 10014, USA
Penguin Books Australia Ltd, Ringwood, Victoria, Australia
Penguin Books Canada Ltd, 10 Alcorn Avenue, Toronto, Ontario, Canada M4V 3B2
Penguin Books (NZ) Ltd, 182–190 Wairau Road, Auckland 10, New Zealand

Penguin Books Ltd, Registered Offices: Harmondsworth, Middlesex, England

First published in this form 1997
1 3 5 7 9 10 8 6 4 2

This translation first published 1954
Copyright © 1954 by Aubrey de Sélincourt, 1954
All rights reserved

Set in 10/13pt Monotype Sabon
Typeset by Rowland Phototypesetting Ltd,
Bury St Edmunds, Suffolk
Printed in England by Clays Ltd, St Ives plc

CONTENTS

Herodotus of Halicarnassus, his *Researches* are here set down to preserve the memory of the past by putting on record the astonishing achievements both of our own and of other peoples; and more particularly, to show how they came into conflict.

The Wife of Candaules

Now Candaules conceived a passion for his own wife, and thought she was the most beautiful woman on earth. So, having in his bodyguard a fellow he particularly liked whose name was Gyges, son of Dascylus, Candaules not only discussed his most important business with him, but even used to make him listen to eulogies of his wife's beauty.

One day the king (who was doomed to a bad end) said to Gyges: 'It appears you don't believe me when I tell you how lovely my wife is. Well, a man always believes his eyes better than his ears; so do as I tell you – contrive to see her naked.'

Gyges gave a cry of horror. 'Master,' he said, 'what an improper suggestion! Do you tell me to look at the queen when she has no clothes on? No, no: "off with her skirt, off with her shame" – you know what they say of women. Let us learn from experience. Right and wrong were distinguished long ago – and I'll tell you one thing that is right: a man should mind his own business. I do not doubt that your wife is the most beautiful of women; so for goodness' sake do not ask me to behave like a criminal.'

Thus he did his utmost to decline the king's invitation, because he was afraid of what might happen if he accepted it.

The king, however, told him not to distress himself. 'There is nothing to be afraid of,' he said, 'either from me or my wife. I am not laying a trap for you; and as for her, I promise she will do you no harm. I'll manage so that she doesn't even know that you have seen her. Look: I will hide you behind the open door of our bedroom. My wife will follow me in to bed. Near the door there's a chair – she will put her clothes on it as takes them off, one by one. You will be able to watch her with perfect ease. Then, while she's walking away from the chair towards the bed with her back to you, slip away through the door – and mind she doesn't catch you.'

Gyges, since he was unable to avoid it, consented, and when bedtime came Candaules brought him to the room. Presently the queen arrived, and Gyges watched her walk in and put her clothes on the chair. Then, just as she had turned her back and was going to bed, he slipped softly out of the room. But the queen saw him.

At once she realized what her husband had done. But

she did not betray the shame she felt by screaming, or even let it appear that she had noticed anything. Instead she silently resolved to have her revenge. For with the Lydians, as with most barbarian races, it is thought highly indecent even for a man to be seen naked.

For the moment she kept her mouth shut and did nothing; but at dawn the next morning she sent for Gyges after preparing the most trustworthy of her servants for what was to come. There was nothing unusual in his being asked to attend upon the queen; so Gyges answered the summons without any suspicion that she knew what had occurred on the previous night.

'Gyges,' she said, as soon as he presented himself, 'there are two courses open to you, and you may take your choice between them. Kill Candaules and seize the throne, with me as your wife; or die yourself on the spot, so that never again may your blind obedience to the king tempt you to see what you have no right to see. One of you must die; either my husband, the author of this wicked plot; or you, who have outraged propriety by seeing me naked.'

For a time Gyges was too much astonished to speak. At last he found words and begged the queen not to force him to make so difficult a choice. But it was no good; he soon saw that he really was faced with the alternatives, either of murdering his master, or of being murdered himself. He made his choice – to live.

'Tell me,' he said, 'since you drive me against my will to kill the king, how shall we set on him?'

'We will attack him when he is asleep,' was the answer; 'and on the very spot where he showed me to you naked.'

All was made ready for the attempt. The queen would not let Gyges go or give him any chance of escaping the dilemma: either Candaules or he must die. Night came, and he followed her into the bedroom. She put a knife into his hand, and hid him behind the same door as before. Then, when Candaules was asleep, he crept from behind the door and struck.

Thus Gyges usurped the throne and married the queen.

Arion and the Dolphin

Periander, who told Thrasybulus about the oracle, was the son of Cypselus, the despot of Corinth. The Corinthians tell of an extraordinary thing that occurred during his life, and the Lesbians confirm the truth of it. It concerns Arion of Methymna, the most distinguished musician of that date, and the man who first, so far as we know, composed and named the dithyramb, and trained choirs to perform it in Corinth. The tale is, that Arion rode on a dolphin's back to Taenarum. Most of his time Arion had spent with Periander, till he felt a longing to sail to Italy and Sicily. This he did; and after making a great deal of money in those countries, he decided to return to Corinth. He sailed from Tarentum in a Corinthian vessel, because he had more confidence in Corinthians than in anyone else. The crew, however, when the ship was at sea, hatched a plot to throw him overboard and steal his money. He got wind of their intention, and begged them to take his money, but spare his life. To no purpose, however; for the sailors told him either to kill himself if he wanted to be buried ashore, or to jump overboard at once.

Arion, seeing they had made up their minds, as a last resource begged permission to stand on the after-deck, dressed in his singing robes, and give them a song; the song over, he promised to kill himself. Delighted at the prospect of hearing a song from the world's most famous singer, the sailors all made their way forward from the stern and assembled amidships. Arion put on his full professional costume, took up his lute and, standing on the after-deck, played and sang a lively tune. Then he leapt into the sea, just as he was, with all his clothes on.

The ship continued her voyage to Corinth, but a dolphin picked up Arion and carried him on its back to Taenarum. Here Arion landed, and made his way in his singing costume to Corinth, where he told the whole story. Periander was not too ready to believe it; so he put Arion under strict supervision, keeping the ship's crew meanwhile carefully in mind. On their return he sent for them, and asked if they had anything to tell him about Arion. 'Oh yes,' they answered, 'we left him safe and sound at Tarentum in Italy.' But no sooner were the words out of their mouths than Arion himself appeared, just as he was when he jumped overboard. This was an unpleasant shock for the sailors. The lie was detected, and further denial was useless.

Lydian Games

I will now say a word about Lydia. The country, unlike some others, has few natural features of much consequence for a historian to describe, except the gold dust which is washed down from Tmolus; it can show, however, the greatest work of human hands in the world, apart from the Egyptian and Babylonian: I mean the tomb of Croesus' father Alyattes. The base of this monument is built of huge stone blocks; the rest of it is a mound of earth. It was raised by the joint labour of the tradesmen, craftsmen and prostitutes, and on the top of it there survived to my own day five stone pillars with inscriptions cut in them to show the amount of work done by each class. Calculation revealed that the prostitutes' share was the largest. Working-class girls in Lydia prostitute themselves without exception to collect money for their dowries, and continue the practice until they marry. They choose their own husbands. The circumference of the tomb is nearly three-quarters of a mile, and its breadth about four hundred yards. Near it is a large lake, the lake of Gyges, said by the Lydians to be never dry. Apart from the fact that they prostitute their daughters, the Lydian way of life is not unlike our own. The Lydians were the first people we know of to use a gold and silver coinage and to introduce retail trade, and they also claim to have invented the games which are now commonly played both by themselves and by the Greeks. These games are supposed to have been invented at the time when they sent a colony to settle in Tyrrhenia, and the story is that in the reign of Atys, the son of Manes, the whole of Lydia suffered from a severe famine. For a time the people lingered on as patiently as they could, but later, when there was no improvement, they began to look for something to alleviate their misery. Various expedients were devised: for instance, the invention of dice, knucklebones and ball-games. In fact they claim to have invented all games of this sort except draughts. The way they used these inventions to help them endure their hunger was to eat and play on alternate days – one day playing so continuously that they had no time to think of food, and eating on the next without playing at all. They managed to live like this for eighteen years. There was still no remission of their suffering – indeed it grew worse; so the king divided the population into two groups and determined by drawing lots which should emigrate and which should remain at home. He appointed himself to rule the section whose lot determined that they should remain, and his son Tyrrhenus to command the emigrants. The lots were drawn, and one section went down to the coast at Smyrna, where they built vessels, put aboard all their household effects and sailed in search of a livelihood elsewhere. They passed many countries and finally reached Umbria in the north of Italy, where they settled and still live to this day. Here they changed their name from Lydians to Tyrrhenians, after the king's son Tyrrhenus, who was their leader.

Ancient Customs

All this I am able to state definitely from personal knowledge. There is another practice, however, concerning the burial of the dead, which is not spoken of openly and is something of a mystery: it is that a male Persian is never buried until the body has been torn by a bird or a dog. I know for certain that the Magi have this custom, for they are quite open about it. The Persians in general, however, cover a body with wax and then bury it. The Magi are a peculiar caste, quite different from the Egyptian priests and indeed from any other sort of person. The Egyptian priests make it an article of religion to kill no living creature except for sacrifice, but the Magi not only kill anything, except dogs and men, with their own hands but make a special point of doing so; ants, snakes, animals, birds – no matter what, they kill them indiscriminately. Well, it is an ancient custom, so let them keep it.

Queen Nitocris

Queen Nitocris was the perpetrator of a grim practical joke. She had a tomb made for herself over one of the main gateways of the city, right high up above the actual entrance, and caused the following inscription to be cut on it: 'If any king of Babylon hereafter is short of money, let him open my tomb and take as much as he likes. But this must be done only in case of need. Whoever opens my tomb under any other circumstances will get no good of it.' The tomb remained undisturbed till the reign of Darius, who resented being unable to use one of the city gates – for he never did use the one under the tomb because, had he done so, he would have had to drive directly under the corpse; moreover, he thought it was absurd, when treasure was lying there asking to be taken, not to take it. So he opened the tomb. He found, however, not a penny inside – but only the body of the queen and another inscription, which read: 'If you had not been insatiably greedy and eager to get money by the most despicable means, you would never have opened the tomb of the dead.' So much, then, for the tradition about the character of Nitocris.

A Sacrifice to Aphrodite

There is one custom among the Babylonians which is wholly shameful: every woman who is a native of the country must once in her life go and sit in the temple of Aphrodite and there give herself to a strange man. Many of the rich women, who are too proud to mix with the rest, drive to the temple in covered carriages with a whole host of servants following behind, and there wait; most, however, sit in the precinct of the temple with a band of plaited string round their heads – and a great crowd they are, what with some sitting there, others arriving, others going away – and through them all gangways are marked off running in every direction for the men to pass along and make their choice. Once a woman has taken her seat she is not allowed to go home until a man has thrown a silver coin into her lap and taken her outside to lie with her. As he throws the coin, the man has to say, 'In the name of the goddess Mylitta' – that being the Assyrian name for Aphrodite. The value of the coin is of no consequence; once thrown it becomes sacred, and the law forbids that it should ever be refused. The woman has no privilege of choice – she must go with the first man who throws her the money. When she has lain with him, her duty to the goddess is discharged and she may go home, after which it will be impossible to seduce her by any offer, however large. Tall, handsome women soon manage to get home again, but the ugly ones stay a long time before they can fulfil the condition which the law demands, some of them, indeed, as much as three or four years. There is a custom similar to this in parts of Cyprus.

The Most Ancient Race

The Egyptians before the reign of Psammetichus used to think that of all races in the world they were the most ancient; Psammetichus, however, when he came to the throne, took it into his head to settle this question of priority, and ever since his time the Egyptians have believed that the Phrygians surpass them in antiquity and that they themselves come second. Psammetichus, finding that mere inquiry failed to reveal which was the original race of mankind, devised an ingenious method of determining the matter. He took at random, from an ordinary family, two newly born infants and gave them to a shepherd to be brought up among his flocks, under strict orders that no one should utter a word in their presence. They were to be kept by themselves in a lonely cottage, and the shepherd was to bring in goats from time to time, to see that the babies had enough milk to drink, and to look after them in any other way that was necessary. All these arrangements were made by Psammetichus because he wished to find out what word the children would first utter, once they had grown out of their meaningless baby-talk. The plan succeeded; two years later the shepherd, who during that time had done everything he had been told to do, happened one day to open the door of the cottage and go in, when both children, running up to him with hands outstretched, pronounced the word 'becos'. The first time this occurred the shepherd made no mention of it; but later, when he found that every time he visited the children to attend to their needs the same word was constantly repeated by them, he informed his master. Psammetichus ordered the children to be brought to him, and when he himself heard them say 'becos' he determined to find out to what language the word belonged. His inquiries revealed that it was the Phrygian for 'bread', and in consideration of this the Egyptians yielded their claims and admitted the superior antiquity of the Phrygians.

Cats, Crocodiles and Hippos

There are not a great many wild animals in Egypt, in spite of the fact that it borders on Libya. Such as there are – both wild and tame – are without exception held to be sacred. To explain the reason for this, I should have to enter into a discussion of religious principles which is a subject I particularly wish to avoid – any slight mention I have already made of such matters having been forced upon me by the needs of my story. But, reasons apart, how they actually behave towards animals I will proceed to describe. The various sorts have guardians appointed for them, sometimes men, sometimes women, who are responsible for feeding them; and the office of guardian is handed down from father to son. Their manner, in the various cities, of performing vows is as follows: praying to the god to whom the particular creature, whichever it may be, is sacred, they shave the heads of their children – sometimes completely, sometimes only a half or a third part – and after weighing the hair in a pair of scales, give an equal weight of silver to the animals' keeper, who then cuts up fish (the animals' usual food) to an equivalent value and gives it to them to eat. Anyone who deliberately kills one of these animals, is punished with death; should one be killed accidentally, the penalty is whatever the priests choose to impose; but for killing an ibis or a hawk, whether deliberately or not, the penalty is inevitably death.

The number, already large, of domestic animals would have been greatly increased, were it not for an odd thing that happens to the cats. The females, when they have kittens, avoid the toms; but the toms, thus deprived of their satisfaction, get over the difficulty very ingeniously, for they either openly seize, or secretly steal, the kittens and kill them – but without eating them – and the result is that the females, deprived of their kittens and wanting more (for their maternal instinct is very strong), go off to look for mates again. What happens when a house catches fire is most extraordinary: nobody takes the least trouble to put it out, for it is only the cats that matter: everyone stands in a row, a little distance from his neighbour, trying to protect the cats, who nevertheless slip through the line, or jump over it, and hurl themselves into the flames. This causes the Egyptians deep distress. All the inmates of a house where a cat has died a natural death shave their eyebrows, and when a dog dies they shave the whole body including the head. Cats which have died are taken to Bubastis, where they are embalmed and buried in sacred receptacles; dogs are buried, also in sacred burial-places, in the towns where they belong. Weasels are buried in the same way as dogs; field-mice and hawks are taken to Buto, ibises to Hermopolis. Bears, which are scarce, and wolves (which in Egypt are not much bigger than jackals) are buried wherever they happen to be found lying dead.

The following is an account of the crocodile. During the four winter months it takes no food. It is a four-footed, amphibious creature, lays and hatches its eggs on land, where it spends the greater part of the day and stays all night in the river, where the water is warmer than the night-air and the dew. The difference in size between the young and the full-grown crocodile is greater than in any other known creature; for a crocodile's egg is hardly bigger than a goose's, and the young when hatched is small in proportion, yet it grows to a size of some twenty-three feet long or even more. It has eyes like a pig's but great fang-like teeth in proportion to its body, and is the only animal to have no tongue and a stationary lower jaw; for when it eats it brings the upper jaw down upon the under. It has powerful claws and a scaly hide, which on its back is impenetrable. It cannot see under water, though on land its sight is remarkably quick. One result of its spending so much time in the water is that the inside of its mouth gets covered with leeches. Other animals avoid the crocodile, as do all birds too with one exception – the sandpiper, or Egyptian plover; this bird is of service to the crocodile and lives, in consequence, in the greatest amity with him; for when the crocodile comes ashore and lies with his mouth wide open (which he generally does facing towards the west), the bird hops in and swallows the leeches. The crocodile enjoys this, and never, in consequence, hurts the bird. Some Egyptians reverence the crocodile as a sacred beast; others do not, but treat it as an enemy. The strongest belief in its sanctity is to be found in Thebes and round about Lake Moeris; in these places they keep one particular crocodile, which they tame, putting rings made of glass or gold into its ears and bracelets round its front feet, and giving it special food and ceremonial offerings. In fact, while these creatures are alive they treat them with every kindness, and, when they die, embalm them and bury them in sacred tombs. On the other hand, in the neighbourhood of Elephantine crocodiles are not considered sacred animals at all, but are eaten. In the Egyptian language these creatures are called *champsae*. The name crocodile – or 'lizard' – was given them by the

Ionians, who saw they resembled the lizards commonly found on stone walls in their own country.

Of the numerous different ways of catching crocodiles I will describe the one which seems to me the most interesting. They bait a hook with a chine of pork and let it float out into midstream, and at the same time, standing on the bank, take a live pig and beat it. The crocodile, hearing its squeals, makes a rush towards it, encounters the bait, gulps it down and is hauled out of the water. The first thing the huntsman does when he has got the beast on land is to plaster its eyes with mud; this done, it is dispatched easily enough – but without this precaution it will give a lot of trouble.

The hippopotamus is held sacred in the district of Papremis, but not elsewhere. This animal has four legs, cloven hoofs like an ox, a snub nose, a horse's mane and tail, conspicuous tusks, a voice like a horse's neigh and is about the size of a very large ox. Its hide is so thick and tough that when dried it can be made into spear-shafts. Otters, too, are found in the Nile; they, and the fish called lepidotus, and eels are all considered sacred to the Nile, as is also the bird known as the fox-goose.

The Phoenix

Another sacred bird is the phoenix; I have not seen a phoenix myself, except in paintings, for it is very rare and visits the country (so at least they say at Heliopolis) only at intervals of 500 years, on the occasion of the death of the parent-bird. To judge by the paintings, its plumage is partly golden, partly red, and in shape and size it is exactly like an eagle. There is a story about the phoenix; it brings its parent in a lump of myrrh all the way from Arabia and buries the body in the temple of the Sun. To perform this feat, the bird first shapes some myrrh into a sort of egg as big as it finds, by testing, that it can carry; then it hollows the lump out, puts its father inside and smears some more myrrh over the hole. The egg-shaped lump is then just of the same weight as it was originally. Finally it is carried by the bird to the temple of the Sun in Egypt. Such, at least, is the story.

The Flying Snakes of Arabia

There is a place in Arabia more or less opposite the city of Buto, where I went to try to get information about the flying snakes. On my arrival I saw their skeletons in incalculable numbers; they were piled in heaps, some of which were big, others smaller, others – the most numerous – smaller still. The place where these bones lie is a narrow mountain pass leading to a broad plain which joins on to the plain of Egypt, and it is said that when the winged snakes fly to Egypt from Arabia in spring, the ibises meet them at the entrance to the pass and do not let them get through, but kill them. According to the Arabians, this service is the reason for the great reverence with which the ibis is regarded in Egypt, and the Egyptians themselves admit the truth of what they say. The ibis is jet-black all over; it has legs like a crane's, a markedly hooked beak and is about the size of a landrail. That, at any rate, is what the black ibis is like – the kind namely that attacks the winged snakes; there is, however, another sort, more commonly found in inhabited districts; this has a bald head and neck and is white except for the head, throat, wing-tips and rump, which are jet-black; its legs and beak are similar to those of the black ibis. The winged snakes resemble watersnakes; their wings are not feathered, but are like a bat's.

Mummies

Mummification is a distinct profession. The embalmers, when a body is brought to them, produce specimen models in wood, painted to resemble nature and graded in quality; the best and more expensive kind is said to represent a being whose name I shrink from mentioning in this connexion; the next best is somewhat inferior and cheaper, while the third sort is cheapest of all. After pointing out these differences in quality, they ask which of the three is required, and the kinsmen of the dead man, having agreed upon a price, go away and leave the embalmers to their work. The most perfect process is as follows: as much as possible of the brain is extracted through the nostrils with an iron hook, and what the hook cannot reach is rinsed out with drugs; next the flank is laid open with a flint knife and the whole contents of the abdomen removed; the cavity is then thoroughly cleansed and washed out, first with palm wine and again with an infusion of pounded spices. After that it is filled with pure bruised myrrh, cassia and every other aromatic substance with the exception of frankincense, and sewn up again, after which the body is placed in natrum, covered entirely over, for seventy days – never longer. When this period, which must not be exceeded, is over, the body is washed and then wrapped from head to foot in linen cut into strips and smeared on the under side with gum, which is commonly used by the Egyptians instead of glue. In this condition, the body is given back to the family, who have a wooden case made, shaped like the human figure, into which it is put. The case is then sealed up and stored in a sepulchral chamber, upright against the wall. When, for reasons of expense, the second quality is called for, the treatment is different: no incision is made and the intestines are not removed, but oil of cedar is injected with a syringe into the body through the anus which is afterwards stopped up to prevent the liquid from escaping. The body is then pickled in natrum for the prescribed number of days, on the last of which the oil is drained off. The effect of it is so powerful that as it leaves the body it brings with it the stomach and intestines in a liquid state, and as the flesh, too, is dissolved by the natrum, nothing of the body is left but the bones and skin. After this treatment it is returned to the family without further fuss.

The third method, used for embalming the bodies of

the poor, is simply to clear out the intestines with a purge and keep the body seventy days in natrum. It is then given back to the family to be taken away.

When the wife of a distinguished man dies, or any woman who happens to be beautiful or well known, her body is not given to the embalmers immediately, but only after the lapse of three or four days. This is a precautionary measure to prevent the embalmers from violating the corpse, a thing which is said actually to have happened in the case of a woman who had just died. The culprit was given away by one of his fellow workmen. If anyone, either an Egyptian or a foreigner, is found drowned in the river or killed by a crocodile, there is the strongest obligation upon the people of the nearest town to have the body embalmed in the most elaborate manner and buried in a consecrated burial-place; no one is allowed to touch it except the priests of the Nile – not even relatives or friends; the priests alone prepare it for burial with their own hands and place it in the tomb, as if it were something more sacred than the body of a man.

The Rage of Pheros

When Sesostris died, he was succeeded by his son Pheros, a prince who undertook no military adventures. He went blind, and the reason for it is explained in the following tale: one year the Nile rose to an excessive height, as much as twenty-seven feet, and when all the fields were under water it began to blow hard, so that the river got very rough. The king in insensate rage seized a spear and hurled it into the swirling waters, and immediately thereafter he was attacked by a disease of the eyes, and became blind. He was blind for ten years, after which he received an oracle from the city of Buto to the effect that the time of his punishment being now ended, he would recover his sight, if he washed his eyes with the urine of a woman who had never lain with any man except her husband. He tried his wife first, but without success – he remained as blind as ever; then he tried other women, a great many, one after another, until at last his sight was restored. Then he collected within the walls of a town, now called Red Clod, all the women except the one whose urine had proved efficacious, set the place on fire and burnt them to death, town and all; afterwards he married the woman who had been the means of curing him. In gratitude for his recovery he dedicated a number of offerings in all the temples of repute; but the most remarkable of them were two stone obelisks which he set up in the precinct of the temple of Hephaestus. These are well worth seeing; they are twelve feet broad and a hundred and fifty feet high, each hewn from a single block of stone.

The Treasure of the King

Rhampsinitus possessed a vast fortune in silver, so great
that no subsequent king came anywhere near it – let alone
surpassed it. In order to keep the treasure safe, he proposed
to have a stone building put up, with one of its walls
forming a part of the outer wall of his palace. The builder
he employed had designs upon the treasure and ingeniously contrived to construct the wall in such a way that
one of the stone blocks of which it was composed could
easily be removed by a couple of men – or even by one.
When the new treasury was ready, the king's money was
stored away in it; and after the lapse of some years the
builder, then on his death-bed, called his two sons and
told them how clever he had been, saying that he had
planned the device of the movable stone entirely for their
benefit, that they might live in affluence. Then he gave
the precise measurements, and instructions for its removal,
and told them that if only they kept the secret well, they
would control the Royal Exchequer as long as they lived.
So the father died and his sons lost no time in setting to

work; they came by night to the palace, found the stone in the treasury wall, took it out easily enough and got away with a good haul of silver. The king, on his next visit to the treasury, was surprised to see that some of the vessels in which the money was stored were no longer full, but as the seals were unbroken and all the locks in perfect order, he was at a loss to find the culprit. When the same thing happened again, and yet again, and he found that each time he visited the chamber the level of the money in the jars had still further fallen (for the thieves persisted in their depredations), he ordered traps to be made and set near the money-jars. The thieves came as usual, and one of them made his way into the chamber; but, as soon as he approached the money-jar he was after, the trap got him. Realizing his plight, he at once called out to his brother to tell him what had happened, and begged him to come in as quickly as he could and cut off his head, lest the recognition of his dead body should involve both of them in ruin. The brother, seeing the sense of this request, acted upon it without delay; then, having fitted the stone back in its place, went home taking the severed head with him. Next morning the king visited his treasury, and what was his astonishment when he saw in the trap the headless body of the thief, and no sign of damage to the building, or any apparent means of entrance or exit! Much perplexed, he finally decided to have the thief's body hung up outside the wall, and a guard set with orders to arrest and bring before him anyone they might see thereabouts in tears, or showing signs of mourning. Now the young man's mother was deeply distressed by this treatment of her dead son's body, and begged the one who was still alive to do all he possibly could to think of some way of getting it back, and even threatened, if he refused to listen to her, to go to the king and denounce him as the thief. The young man made many excuses, but to no purpose; his mother continued to pester him, until at last he thought of a way out of the difficulty. He filled some skins with wine and loaded them on to donkeys, which he drove to the place where the soldiers were guarding his brother's corpse. Arrived there, he gave a pull on the necks of two or three of the skins, which undid the fastenings. The wine poured out, and he roared and banged his head, as if not knowing which donkey to deal with first, while the soldiers, seeing the wine streaming all over the road, seized their pots and ran to catch it, congratulating themselves on such a piece of luck. The young man swore at them in pretended rage, which the soldiers did their best to soothe, until finally he changed his tune, and, appearing to have recovered his temper, drove the donkeys out of the roadway and began to rearrange the wine-skins on their backs. Meanwhile, as he chatted with the soldiers, one of them cracked a joke at his expense and made him laugh, whereupon he made them a present of a wine-skin, and without more ado they all sat down to enjoy themselves, and urged their benefactor to join the party and share the drink. The young man let himself be persuaded, and soon, as cup succeeded cup and the soldiers treated him with increasing familiarity, he gave them another skin. Such a quantity of wine was too much for the guards; very drunk and drowsy, they stretched themselves out at full length and fell asleep on the spot. It was now well after dark, and the thief took down his brother's body and as an insult shaved the right cheek of each of the guards. Then he put the corpse on the donkeys' backs and returned home, having done successfully what his mother demanded.

The king was very angry when he learnt that the thief's body had been stolen, and determined at any cost to catch the man who had been clever enough to bring off such a coup. I find it hard to believe the priests' account of the means he employed to catch him – but here it is: he sent his own daughter to a brothel with orders to admit all comers, and to compel each applicant, before granting him her favours, to tell her what was the cleverest and wickedest thing that he had ever done; and if anyone told her the story of the thief, she was to get hold of him and not allow him to escape. The girl obeyed her father's orders, and the thief, when he came to know the reason for what she was doing, could not resist the temptation to go one better than the king in ingenuity. He cut the hand and arm from the body of a man who had just died, and, putting them under his cloak, went to visit the king's daughter in her brothel. When she asked him the question which she had asked all the others, he replied that his wickedest deed was to cut off his brother's head when he was caught in a trap in the king's treasury, and his cleverest was to make the soldiers drunk, so that he could take down his brother's body from the wall where it was hanging. The girl immediately clutched at him; but under cover of the darkness the thief pushed towards her the hand of the corpse, which she seized and held tight in the belief that it was his own. Then, leaving it in her grasp, he made his escape through the door.

The cleverness and audacity of this last exploit filled the king with astonishment and admiration; soon after the news of it reached him, he went to every town in

Egypt with a promise to the thief, should he give himself up, not only of a free pardon but of a rich reward. The thief trusted him and presented himself, and Rhampsinitus signalized his admiration for the most intelligent of all mankind by giving him his daughter in marriage. The Egyptians, he said, were the cleverest nation in the world, but this fellow beat the lot.

Sethos and Sennacherib

Next on the throne after Anysis was Sethos, the high priest of Hephaestus. He is said to have neglected the warrior class of the Egyptians and to have treated them with contempt, as if he had been unlikely to need their services. He offended them in various ways, not least by depriving them of the twelve acres of land which each of them had held by special privilege under previous kings. As a result, when Egypt was invaded by Sennacherib, the king of Arabia and Assyria, with a great army, not one of them was willing to fight. The situation was grave; not knowing what else to do, the priest-king entered the shrine and, before the image of the god, complained bitterly of the peril which threatened him. In the midst of his lamentations he fell asleep, and dreamt that the god stood by him and urged him not to lose heart; for it he marched boldly out to meet the Arabian army, he would come to no harm, as the god himself would send him helpers.

By this dream the king's confidence was restored; and with such men as were willing to follow him – not a single one of the warrior class, but a mixed company of shopkeepers, artisans and market-people – he marched to Pelusium, which guards the approaches to Egypt, and there took up his position. As he lay here facing the Assyrians, thousands of field-mice swarmed over them during the night, and ate their quivers, their bowstrings and the leather handles of their shields, so that on the following day, having no arms to fight with, they abandoned their position and suffered severe losses during their retreat. There is still a stone statue of Sethos in the temple of Hephaestus; the figure is represented with a mouse in its hand, and the inscription: 'Look upon me and learn reverence.'

The Egyptian Labyrinth

After the reign of Sethos, the priest of Hephaestus, the Egyptians for a time were freed from monarchical government. Unable, however, to do without a king, for long they divided Egypt into twelve regions and appointed a king for each of them. United by intermarriage, the twelve kings governed in mutual friendliness on the understanding that none of them should attempt to oust any of the others, or to increase his power at the expense of the rest. They came to the understanding, and ensured that the terms of it should be rigorously kept, because, at the time when the twelve kingdoms were first established, an oracle had declared that the one who should pour a libation from a bronze cup in the temple of Hephaestus would become master of all Egypt. They held their meetings in all the temples.

To strengthen the bond between them, they decided to leave a common memorial of their reigns, and for this purpose constructed a labyrinth a little above Lake Moeris, near the place called the City of Crocodiles. I have seen this building, and it is beyond my power to describe; it must have cost more in labour and money than all the walls and public works of the Greeks put together – though no one would deny that the temples at Ephesus and Samos are remarkable buildings. The pyramids, too, are astonishing structures, each one of them equal to many of the most ambitious works of Greece; but the labyrinth surpasses them. It has twelve covered courts – six in a row facing north, six south – the gates of the one range exactly fronting the gates of the other, with a continuous wall round the outside of the whole. Inside, the building is of two storeys and contains three thousand rooms, of which half are underground, and the other half directly above them. I was taken through the rooms in the upper storey, so what I shall say of them is from my own observation, but the underground ones I can speak of only from report, because the Egyptians in charge refused to let me see them, as they contain the tombs of the kings who built the labyrinth, and also the tombs of the sacred crocodiles. The upper rooms, on the contrary, I did actually see, and it is hard to believe that they are the work of men; the baffling and intricate passages from room to room and from court to court were an endless wonder to me, as we passed from a courtyard into rooms, from rooms into galleries, from galleries into more rooms and thence into yet more courtyards. The roof of every chamber, courtyard, and gallery is, like the walls, of stone. The walls are covered with carved figures, and each court is exquisitely built of white marble and surrounded by a colonnade. Near the corner where the labyrinth ends there is a pyramid, two hundred and forty feet in height, with great carved figures of animals on it and an underground passage by which it can be entered.

The Nature of Skulls

At the place where this battle was fought I saw a very odd thing, which the natives had told me about. The bones still lay there, those of the Persian dead separate from those of the Egyptians, just as they were originally divided, and I noticed that the skulls of the Persians are so thin that the merest touch with a pebble will pierce them, but those of the Egyptians, on the other hand, are so tough that it is hardly possible to break them with a blow from a stone. I was told, very credibly, that the reason was that the Egyptians shave their heads from childhood, so that the bone of the skull is indurated by the action of the sun – this is also why they hardly ever go bald, baldness being rarer in Egypt than anywhere else. This, then, explains the thickness of their skulls; and the thinness of the Persians' skulls rests upon a similar principle: namely that they have always worn felt skull-caps, to guard their heads from the sun. I also observed the same thing at Papremis, where the Persians serving under Achaemenes, the son of Darius, were destroyed by Inarus the Libyan.

Cambyses and the Fish-Eaters

Cambyses made plans for three separate military ventures: one against the Carthaginians, another against the Ammonians and the third against the long-lived Ethiopians, on the coast of the Indian Ocean, south of Libya. He proposed to send his fleet against the Carthaginians and a part of his land forces against the Ammonians; to Ethiopia he decided first to send spies, ostensibly with presents to the king, but actually to collect what information they could; in particular he wanted them to find out if the so-called Table of the Sun really existed. (The story about the Table of the Sun is that there is a meadow, situated in the outskirts of the city, where a plentiful supply of boiled meat of all kinds is kept; it is the duty of the magistrates to put the meat there at night, and during the day anybody who wishes may come and eat it. Local legend has it that the meat appears spontaneously and is the gift of the earth.)

Having decided that the spies should go, Cambyses sent to Elephantine for some men of the Fish-Eaters who were acquainted with the Ethiopian language, and, while they were being fetched, gave orders for the fleet to sail against Carthage. The Phoenicians, however, refused to go, because of the close bond which connected Phoenicia and Carthage, and the wickedness of making war against their own children. In this way, with the Phoenicians out of it and the remainder of the naval force too weak to undertake the campaign alone, the Carthaginians escaped Persian domination. Cambyses did not think fit to bring pressure to bear, because the Phoenicians had taken service under him of their own free will, and his whole naval power was dependent on them. The Cyprians, too, had given their services to Persia and took part in the Egyptian campaign.

The Fish-Eaters who had been summoned from Elephantine were sent off to Ethiopia with instructions on what they were to say on their arrival: they took with them as presents for the king a scarlet robe, a gold chain-necklace and bracelets, an alabaster casket of myrrh and a jar of palm-wine. The Ethiopians, who were the objects of all this attention, are said to be the tallest and best-looking people in the world. Their laws and customs are peculiar to themselves, and the strangest is the method they have of choosing for their king the man whom they judge to be the tallest, and strong in proportion to his height. The Fish-Eaters duly arrived in the country and presented their gifts to the king with the following words: 'Cambyses, King of Persia, wishing to be your friend and guest, has sent us here with orders to have speech with you, and these gifts he offers you are just the things which he himself takes most pleasure in using.'

But the Ethiopian king knew the men were spies, and answered: 'The king of Persia has not sent you with these presents because he puts a high value upon being my friend. You have come to get information about my kingdom; therefore, you are liars, and that king of yours is a bad man. Had he any respect for what is right, he would not have coveted any other kingdom than his own, nor made slaves of a people who have done him no wrong. So take him this bow, and tell him that the king of Ethiopia has some advice to give him: when the Persians can draw a bow of this size thus easily, then let him raise an army of superior strength and invade the country of the long-lived Ethiopians. Till then, let him thank the gods for not turning the thoughts of the children of Ethiopia to foreign conquest.' He then unstrung the bow, put it into the hands of the Fish-Eaters and picked up the scarlet robe, asking what it was and how it was made. The men explained about the dye and how the material was dipped in it, whereupon the king replied that both the dyers and the garments they dyed were pretending to be what they were not, and were therefore cheats. Then he asked about the gold chain and the bracelets, and when the Fish-Eaters explained their use as ornaments he laughed and, supposing them to be fetters, remarked that they had stronger ones in their own country. Next he asked about the myrrh, and after hearing how it was prepared and how people rubbed it on their bodies for a perfume, he repeated the comment he had made about the scarlet robe. Finally he came to the wine and, having learnt the process of its manufacture, drank some and found it delicious; then, for a last question, he asked what the Persian king ate and what was the greatest age that Persians could attain. Getting in reply an account of the nature and cultivation of wheat, and hearing that the Persian king ate bread, and that people in Persia did not commonly live beyond eighty, he said he was not surprised that anyone who ate dung should die so soon, adding that Persians would doubtless die younger still, if they did not keep themselves going with that drink – and here he pointed to the wine, the one thing in which he admitted the superiority of the Persians.

The Fish-Eaters, in their turn, asked the king how long the Ethiopians lived and what they ate, and were told that most of them lived to be a hundred and twenty, and some even more, and that they ate boiled meat and drank milk. When they expressed surprise that anyone should live to such an advanced age, they were taken to a spring, the water from which smelt like violets and caused a man's skin, when he washed in it, to glisten as if he had washed in oil. They said the water of this spring lacked density to such a degree that nothing would float in it, neither wood nor any lighter substance – everything sank to the bottom. If this account is true, then their constant use of it must be the cause of the Ethiopians' longevity. After the visit to the spring the king conducted them to a prison in which all the prisoners were bound with gold chains – for in Ethiopia the rarest and most precious metal is bronze. Inspection of the prison was followed by inspection of the Table of the Sun, and last of all they were taken to see the coffins. These coffins are said to be made of crystal, and the method the Ethiopians follow is first to dry the corpse, either by the Egyptian process or some other, then cover it all over with gypsum and paint it to resemble as closely as possible the living man; then they enclose it in a shaft of crystal which has been hollowed out, like a cylinder, to receive it. The stuff is easily worked and is mined in large quantities. The corpse is plainly visible inside the cylinder; there is no disagreeable smell, or any other cause of annoyance, and every detail can be as distinctly seen as if there were nothing between one's eyes and the body. The next-of-kin keep the cylinder in their houses for a year, offering it the first fruits and sacrificing to it; then they carry it out and set it up near the town.

Having now seen all they could, the spies returned to Egypt to make their report, which so angered Cambyses that he at once began his march against Ethiopia, without any orders for the provision of supplies, and without for a moment considering the fact that he was to take his men to the ends of the earth. He lost his wits completely and, like the madman he was, the moment he heard what the Fish-Eaters had to say, off he went with his whole force of infantry, leaving behind the Greeks who were serving under him. Arrived at Thebes, he detached a body of 50,000 men with orders to attack the Ammonians, reduce them to slavery and burn the oracle of Zeus; then with his remaining forces he continued his march towards Ethiopia. They had not, however, covered a fifth of the distance, when everything in the nature of provisions gave out, and the men were forced to eat the pack-animals until they, too, were all gone. If Cambyses, when he saw what the situation was, had changed his mind and returned to his base, he would, in spite of his original error, have shown some sense; but as it was, he paid not the least attention to what was happening and continued his advance. The troops kept themselves alive by eating green-stuff so long as there was any to be had in the country, but once they had reached the desert, some of them were reduced to the dreadful expedient of cannibalism. One man in ten was chosen by lot to be the victim. This was too much even for Cambyses; when it was reported to him, he abandoned the expedition, marched back and arrived at Thebes with greatly reduced numbers. From Thebes he went down to Memphis and allowed the Greeks to sail home. So ended the expedition against Ethiopia.

The Ring of Polycrates

While Cambyses was occupied with the Egyptian expedition, the Lacedaemonians made an expedition to Samos against Polycrates, the son of Aeces. Polycrates had seized power in the island, and at the outset had divided his realm into three and gone shares with his brothers, Pantagnotus and Syloson; later, however, he killed the former, banished the latter (the younger of the two) and held the whole island himself. Once master of it, he concluded a pact of friendship with Amasis, king of Egypt, sealing it by a mutual exchange of presents. It was not long before the rapid increase of his power became the talk of Ionia and the rest of Greece. All his campaigns were victorious, his every venture a success. He had a fleet of a hundred fifty-oared galleys and a force of a thousand bowmen. His plundering raids were widespread and indiscriminate – he used to say that a friend would be more grateful if he gave him back what he had taken, than if he had never taken it. He captured many of the islands and a number of towns on the mainland as well. Among other successes, he defeated at sea the Lesbians, who had sent their whole fleet to the help of Miletus; the prisoners he took were forced to dig, in chains, the whole moat which surrounds the walls of Samos.

Amasis was fully aware of the remarkable luck which Polycrates enjoyed, and it caused him some uneasiness; accordingly when he heard of his ever-mounting tale of successes, he wrote him the following letter, and sent it to Samos: 'Amasis to Polycrates: – It is a pleasure to hear of a friend and ally doing well, but, as I know that the gods are jealous of success, I cannot rejoice at your excessive prosperity. My own wish, both for myself and for those I care for, would be to do well in some things and badly in others, passing through life with alternate success and failure; for I have never yet heard of a man who after an unbroken run of luck was not finally brought to complete ruin. Now I suggest that you deal with the danger of your continual successes in the following way: think of whatever it is you value most – whatever you would most regret the loss of – and throw it away: throw it right away, so that nobody can ever see it again. If, after that, you do not find that success alternates with failure, then go on using the remedy I have advised.'

Polycrates read the letter and approved of the advice

which it contained; so he began to look around among his treasures for what he felt he would be most grieved to lose, and finally hit upon a ring. This was a signet-ring he used to wear, an emerald set in gold, the work of a Samian named Theodorus, the son of Telecles. Having decided that this was the thing to get rid of, he manned a galley, went aboard and gave orders to put to sea. When the vessel was a long way off-shore, he took the ring from his finger, in full view of everyone on board, and threw it into the water. Then he rowed back to the island, returned to his house, and lamented his lost treasure.

Five or six days later it happened that a fisherman caught a fine big fish and thought it would make a worthy present for Polycrates. He took it to the door and asked for an audience; this being granted, he offered the fish, and said: 'My King, I did not think it right to take this fish I caught to market, poor working man though I am; it is such a fine one that I thought it good enough for you and your greatness. So I have brought it here to give you.'

Polycrates, much pleased with what the fisherman said, replied: 'You have done very well, and I thank you twice over – once for your words, and again for your present. I invite you to take supper with me.'

The fisherman then went home, very proud of the

honour done him. Meanwhile Polycrates' servants cut up the fish, and found the signet-ring in its belly. The moment they saw it, they picked it up, and taking it to Polycrates in triumph, told him how it had been found. Seeing in this the hand of providence, Polycrates wrote a letter to Amasis in Egypt, and related to him everything he had done and what the result had been. Amasis read the letter, and at once replied how impossible it is for one man to save another from his destiny, and how certain it was that Polycrates, whose luck held even to the point of finding again what he deliberately threw away, would one day die a miserable death. He forthwith sent a messenger to Samos to say that the pact between Polycrates and himself was at an end. This he did in order that when the destined calamity fell upon Polycrates, he might avoid the distress he would have felt, had Polycrates still been his friend.

The Gold-Digging Ants

There are other Indians further north, round the city of Caspatyrus and in the country of Pactyica, who in their mode of life resemble the Bactrians. These are the most warlike of the Indian tribes, and it is they who go out to fetch the gold – for in this region there is a sandy desert. There is found in this desert a kind of ant of great size – bigger than a fox, though not so big as a dog. Some specimens, which were caught there, are kept at the palace of the Persian king. These creatures as they burrow underground throw up the sand in heaps, just as our own ants throw up the earth, and they are very like ours in shape. The sand has a rich content of gold, and this it is that the Indians are after when they make their expeditions into the desert. Each man harnesses three camels abreast, a female, on which he rides, in the middle, and a male on each side in a leading-rein, and takes care that the female is one who has as recently as possible dropped her young. Their camels are as fast as horses, and much more powerful carriers. There is no need for me to describe the camel, for the Greeks are familiar with what it looks like; one thing, however, I will mention, which will be news to them: the camel in its hind legs has four thighs and four knees, and its genitals point backwards towards its tail. That, then, is how these Indians equip themselves for the expedition, and they plan their time-table so as actually to get their hands on the gold during the hottest part of the day, when the heat will have driven the ants underground. In this part of the world the sun is not, as it is elsewhere, hottest at noon, but in the morning: from dawn, that is, until closing-time in the market. During this part of the day the heat is much fiercer than it is at noon in Greece, and the natives are said to soak themselves in water to make it endurable. At midday the heat diminishes and is much the same here as elsewhere, and, as the afternoon goes on, it becomes about equal to what one finds in other countries in the early morning. Towards evening it grows cooler and cooler, until at sunset it is really cold.

When the Indians reach the place where the gold is, they fill the bags they have brought with them with sand, and start for home again as fast as they can go; for the ants (if we may believe the Persians' story) smell them and at once give chase; nothing in the world can touch these ants for speed, so not one of the Indians would get home alive, if they did not make sure of a good start while the ants were mustering their forces. The male camels, who are slower movers than the females, soon begin to drag and are left behind, one after the other, while the females are kept going hard by the memory of their young, who were left at home.

Spices and Sheep

It would seem to be a fact that the remotest parts of the world have the finest products, whereas Greece has far the best and most temperate climate. The most easterly country in the inhabited world is India; and here both animals and birds are much bigger than elsewhere – if we except the Indian horse, which is inferior in size to the Median breed known as the Nisaean. Gold, too, is found here in immense quantity, either mined, or washed down by rivers, or stolen from the ants in the manner I have described; and there are trees growing wild which produce a kind of wool better than sheep's wool in beauty and quality, which the Indians use for making their clothes. The most southerly country is Arabia; and Arabia is the only place that produces frankincense, myrrh, cassia, cinnamon and the gum called ledanon. All these, except the myrrh, cause the Arabians a lot of trouble to collect. When they gather frankincense, they burn storax (the gum which is brought into Greece by the Phoenicians) in order to raise a smoke to drive off the flying snakes; these snakes, the same which attempt to invade Egypt, are small in size and of various colours, and great numbers of them keep guard over all the trees which bear the frankincense, and the only way to get rid of them is by smoking them out with storax. The Arabians say that the whole world would swarm with these creatures were it not for a certain peculiar fact – the same thing, incidentally, as keeps down the spread of adders. And indeed it is hard to avoid the belief that divine providence, in the wisdom that one would expect of it, has made prolific every kind of creature which is timid and preyed upon by others, in order to ensure its continuance, while savage and noxious species are comparatively unproductive. Hares, for instance, which are the prey of all sorts of animals, not to mention birds and men, are excessively prolific; they are the only animals in which superfetation occurs, and you will find in a hare's womb young in all stages of development, some with fur on, others with none, others just beginning to form, and others, again, barely conceived. A lioness, on the contrary, the most bold and powerful of beasts, produces but a single cub, once in her life – for she expels from her body not only the cub, but her womb as well – or what is left of it. The reason for this is that when the unborn cub begins to stir, he scratches at the walls of the womb with his claws, which are sharper than any other animal's, and as he grows bigger scrabbles his way further and further through them until by the time he is about to be born, the womb is almost wholly destroyed. In the same way, if adders and the Arabian flying snakes were able to replace themselves naturally, it would be impossible for men to live. Fortunately, however, they are not; for when they couple, the female seizes the male by the neck at the very moment of the release of the sperm, and hangs on until she has bitten it through. That finishes the male; and the female, too, has to pay for her behaviour, for the young in her belly avenge their father by gnawing at her insides, until they end by eating their way out. Other species of snakes, which are harmless to men, lay eggs and hatch out their young in large numbers. The reason why flying snakes seem so numerous in Arabia is that they are all concentrated in that country – you will not find them anywhere else, whereas adders are common all over the world.

When the Arabians go out to collect cassia, they cover their bodies and faces, all but their eyes, with ox-hides and other skins. The plant grows in a shallow lake which, together with the ground round about it, is infested by winged creatures like bats, which screech alarmingly and are very pugnacious. They have to be kept from attacking the men's eyes while they are cutting the cassia. The process of collecting cinnamon is still more remarkable. Where it comes from and what country produces it, they do not know; the best some of them can do is to make a fair guess that it grows somewhere in the region where Dionysus was brought up. What they say is that the dry sticks, which we have learnt from the Phoenicians to call cinnamon, are brought by large birds, which carry them to their nests, made of mud, on mountain precipices, which no man can climb, and that the method the Arabians have invented for getting hold of them is to cut up the bodies of dead oxen, or donkeys, or other animals into very large joints, which they carry to the spot in question and leave on the ground near the nests. They then retire to a safe distance and the birds fly down and carry off the joints of meat to their nests, which, not being strong enough to bear the weight, break and fall to the ground. Then the men come along and pick up the cinnamon, which is subsequently exported to other countries. Still more surprising is the way of getting ledanon – or ladanon, as the Arabians call it. Sweet-smelling substance though it is, it is found in a most malodorous place; sticking, namely, like glue in the beards of he-goats who have been browsing among the bushes. It is used as an ingredient in many kinds of perfume, and is what the Arabians chiefly burn as incense.

So much for the perfumes: let me only add that the whole country exhales a more than earthly fragrance. One other thing is remarkable enough to deserve a mention – the sheep. There are two kinds, such as are found nowhere else; one kind has such long tails – not less than 4½ feet – that if they were allowed to trail on the ground, they would develop sores from the constant friction; so to obviate this, the shepherds have devised the art of making little carts of wood, and fix one of them under the tail of each sheep. The other kind have flat tails, eighteen inches broad.

Darius and Domocedes

Darius was out hunting and happened to twist his foot
as he dismounted from his horse. The injury was serious,
the ankle being actually dislocated. It had been his custom
for some time to keep in attendance certain Egyptian
doctors, who had a reputation for the highest eminence
in their profession, and these men he now consulted. But
in their efforts to reduce the joint, they wrenched the foot
so clumsily that they only made matters worse. For seven
days and nights Darius was unable to sleep for pain, and
was very ill; on the eighth day, however, being informed
about the skill of Democedes of Crotona by someone who
had previously heard of him in Sardis, he ordered him to
be fetched immediately. The man was found in a neglected
condition among Oroetes' slaves, and brought to the
palace just as he was, dressed in rags and dragging his
chains. When he came into the royal presence and Darius
asked him if he understood the art of medicine, he replied
that he did not, for he was afraid that if he declared
himself he would never be allowed to return home to

Greece. Darius, however, was not deceived; realizing that Democedes was concealing his knowledge, he told the men who had brought him to fetch the whips and the iron spikes. This was enough to force an admission – up to a point; for Democedes still maintained that he had no thorough medical knowledge, but had merely acquired a smattering of it by living with a doctor. All the same, Darius put himself in his hands, and Democedes, by using Greek methods and substituting milder remedies for the rough-and-ready treatment of the Egyptian doctors, enabled the king to get some sleep, and very soon cured him completely. Darius, who had never expected to be able to use his foot again, presented him with two sets of gold chains, a gift which caused Democedes to ask if the king was determined to double his sufferings as a reward for the cure he had effected. This amused Darius, who thereupon sent him off to visit his wives, and when the eunuchs who conducted him to their apartments told them that this was the man who had saved the king's life, they each scooped a cupful of gold coins from a chest and gave them to Democedes. There was such a lot of money that a servant called Sciton, by picking up the coins which spilt over the cups, managed to collect quite a fortune.

The Soothsayers of Scythia

There are many soothsayers in Scythia, and their method is to work with willow rods. They bring great bundles of them, which they put down on the ground; then they untie them, lay out each rod separately and pronounce their prophecy. While they are speaking it, they collect the rods into a bundle again as before. This is the native mode of divination in Scythia; but the class of effeminate persons called 'Enarees' use a different method, which they say was taught them by Aphrodite: these people take a piece of the inner bark of the lime-tree and cut it into three pieces, which they keep twisting and untwisting round their fingers as they prophesy.

When the king of Scythia falls sick, he sends for three of the most reputable soothsayers, who proceed to practise their arts in the way I have described; more often than not they declare that such and such a person (whose name they mention) has sworn falsely by the king's hearth – it being customary in Scythia to use this form of oath for the most solemn purposes. The supposed culprit is at once arrested and brought into the king's presence, where he is charged by the soothsayers, who tell him that their powers of divination have revealed that he has sworn by the king's hearth and perjured himself, and that his perjury is the cause of the king's sickness. The man, of course, denies the charge, and makes a great fuss, whereupon the king sends for more soothsayers – six this time instead of three – who also bring their skill to bear. Should they convict the accused of perjury, he is beheaded without more ado, and his property is divided by lot among the first three soothsayers; if, however, the new six acquit him, more are brought in, and, if need be, still more again, and if, in the final result, the majority declare for the man's innocence, the law is that the three original ones should be executed. The method of execution is this: a cart is filled with sticks and harnessed to oxen; the guilty men, gagged and bound hand and foot, are thrust down among the sticks, which are then set alight, and the oxen scared off at a run. Often the oxen are burnt to death together with the soothsayers; often, too, the pole of the cart is burnt through soon enough to allow them to escape with a scorching. Peccant soothsayers – 'lying prophets' as they are called – are burnt to death in this way for other crimes besides the one I have described. When the king orders an execution, he does not allow the criminal's sons to survive him: all males are put to death, but not the females, who are in no way harmed.

The Crime of Anacharsis

Like the Egyptians, the Scythians are dead-set against foreign ways, especially against Greek ways. An illustration of this is what happened to Anacharsis – and, later, to Scylas. The former was a great traveller, and a man of great and varied knowledge; he had given proof of this in many parts of the world, and was on his way home to Scythia when, as he was passing through the Hellespont, he broke his journey at Cyzicus. Finding the people of this town engaged in celebrating a magnificent festival in honour of the Mother of the Gods, Anacharsis made a vow that, if he got home safe and sound, he would himself celebrate a night-festival and offer sacrifice to this goddess in exactly the same way as he had seen it done at Cyzicus. On his arrival in Scythia, he entered the Woodland – that forest of all sorts of trees, which lies near Achilles' Racecourse – and, according to his promise, went through the ceremony with all the proper rites and observances, drum in hand and the images fastened to his dress. He happened to be noticed by some Scythian or other, who at once went and told Saulius, the king; Saulius then came in person, and, seeing Anacharsis occupied with these outlandish rites, shot him dead. Today, if anyone asks about Anacharsis, the Scythians say they never heard of him – all because he travelled abroad into Greece and adopted foreign practices. But as I was told by Tymnes, the agent of Ariapithes, Anacharsis was the uncle of the Scythian king Idanthyrsus, and son of Gnurus, grandson of Lycus, and great-grandson of Spargapithes. If he was really a member of this family, he must have been killed by his own brother; for Idanthyrus was a son of Saulius, and it was Saulius who shot him. There is also a different story about Anacharsis which I have heard in the Peloponnese; according to this, he was sent abroad by the king of Scythia to find out what he could about Greece, and told the king on his return that all the Greeks were too busy to study any branch of learning, with the sole exception of the Lacedaemonians, who were the only ones to be able to keep up a sensible conversation. This story, however, is only a frivolous Greek invention; the plain truth is that Anacharsis was killed in the way I have described, for associating with Greeks and adopting foreign ways.

The Destroying Wind

The neighbours of the Nasamones are the Psylli – but they no longer exist. There is a story which I repeat as the Libyans tell it; that the south wind dried up the water in their storage tanks, so that they were left with none whatever, as their territory lies wholly within the Syrtis. Upon this they held a council, and having unanimously decided to declare war on the south wind, they marched out to the desert, where the wind blew and buried them in sand. The whole tribe was wiped out, and the Nasamones occupied their former domain.

Hunting the Troglodytes

Ten days' journey west of the Ammonians, along the belt of sand, there is a salt-hill and spring. This place, called Augila, is also inhabited, and it is here that the Nasamonians come for their date harvest. Again at the same distance to the west is a salt-hill and spring, just as before, with date-palms of the fruit-bearing kind, as in the other oases; and here live the Garamantes, a very numerous tribe of people, who spread soil over the salt to sow their seed in. From these people is the shortest route – thirty days' journey – to the Lotophagi; and it is among them that the cattle are found which walk backwards as they graze. The reason for this curious habit is provided by the formation of their horns, which bend forwards and downwards; this prevents them from moving forwards in the ordinary way, for, if they tried to do so, their horns would stick in the ground. In other respects they are just like ordinary cattle – except for the thickness and toughness of their hide. The Garamantes hunt the Ethiopian hole-men, or troglodytes, in four-horse chariots, for these troglodytes are exceedingly swift of foot – more so than any people of whom we have any information. They eat snakes and lizards and other reptiles and speak a language like no other, but squeak like bats.

The Pillar of the Sky

Ten days' journey from the Garamantes is yet another hill and spring – this time the home of the Atarantes, the only people in the world, so far as our knowledge goes, to do without names. Atarantes is the collective name – but individually they have none. They curse the sun as it rises and call it by all sorts of opprobrious names, because it wastes and burns both themselves and their land. Once more at a distance of ten days' journey there is a salt-hill, a spring and a tract of inhabited country, and adjoining it rises Mount Atlas. In shape the mountain is a slender cone, and it is so high that according to report the top cannot be seen, because summer and winter it is never free of cloud. The natives (who are known as the Atlantes, after the mountains) call it the Pillar of the Sky. They are said to eat no living creature, and never to dream.

The Libyans

The coast of Libya between Egypt and Lake Tritonis is occupied by nomads living on meat and milk – though they do not breed pigs, and abstain from cows' meat for the same reason as the Egyptians. Even at Cyrene women think it is wrong to eat cows' meat, out of respect for the Egyptian Isis, in whose honour they celebrate both fasts and festivals. At Barca the women avoid eating pigs' flesh, as well as cows'. West of Tritonis, nomad tribes are no longer found; the people are quite different, not only in their general way of life, but in the treatment of their children. Many of the nomads – perhaps all, but I cannot be certain about this – when their children are four years old, burn the veins on their heads, and sometimes on their temples, with a bit of greasy wool, as a permanent cure for catarrh. For this reason they are said to be the healthiest people in the world – indeed, it is true enough that they are healthier than any other race we know of, though I should not care to be too certain that this is the reason. Anyway, about the fact of their health there is no doubt.

Should the cauterizing of the veins bring on convulsions, they have discovered that the effective remedy is to sprinkle goat's urine on the child – I repeat in all this what is said by the Libyans. When the nomad tribes sacrifice, the process is to begin by cutting off the victim's ear, which they throw over the house as a preliminary offering, and then to wring the animal's neck. They sacrifice to the sun and moon, the worship of which is common to all the Libyans, though those who live round Lake Tritonis sacrifice chiefly to Athene, and, after her, to Triton and Poseidon ... The nomad Libyans – except the Nasamonians – bury their dead just as we do in Greece; the Nasamonians, however, bury them in a sitting position, and take care when anyone is dying to make him sit up, and not to let him die flat on his back. Their houses, which are portable, are made of the dry haulms of some plant, knit together with rush ropes.

The Dog-Headed Men

West of the Triton, and beyond the Auses, Libya is inhabited by tribes who live in ordinary houses and practise agriculture. First come the Maxyes, a people who grow their hair on the right side of their heads and shave it off on the left. They stain their bodies red and claim to be descended from the men of Troy. The country round here, and the rest of Libya to the westward, has more forest and a greater number of wild animals than the region which the nomads occupy. The latter — that is, eastern Libya — is low-lying and sandy as far as the river Triton, whereas the agricultural region to the west is very hilly, and abounds with forest and animal life. It is here that the huge snakes are found — and lions, elephants, bears, asps and horned asses, not to mention dog-headed men, headless men with eyes in their breasts (I don't vouch for this, but merely repeat what the Libyans say), wild men and wild women and a great many other creatures by no means of a fabulous kind. In the nomads' country none of these occur; instead, one finds white-rump antelopes, gazelles, deer, asses – not the horned sort but a different species which can do without water; it is a fact that they do not drink – another kind of antelope, about as big as an ox, the horns of which are used for making the curved sides of lyres, foxes, hyaenas, hedgehogs, wild rams, jackals, panthers and others, including land-crocodiles like huge lizards, four and a half feet long, ostriches and small snakes with a single horn. All these are found, together with other animals common elsewhere, with the exception of the stag and the wild boar, of which there are none at all in Libya. There are, however, three kinds of mice, called respectively *dipodes*, *zegeries*, and *echines* – also weasels which are found among the silphium, and resemble those at Tartessus. So much, then, for the animal life in that part of Libya where the nomads are: I have made it as full and accurate as my extensive inquiries permit.

A Thracian Custom

With the Thracians who live beyond Creston, it is customary for a man to have a number of wives; and when a husband dies, his wives enter into keen competition, in which his friends play a vigorous part on one side or the other, to decide which of them was most loved. The one on whom the honour of the verdict falls is first praised by both men and women, and then slaughtered over the grave by her next of kin and buried by her husband's side. For the other wives, not to be chosen is the worst possible disgrace, and they grieve accordingly.

Hippocleides

Cleisthenes, the son of Aristonymus, grandson of Myron, and great-grandson of Andreas, had a daughter, Agarista, whom he wished to marry to the best man in all Greece. So during the Olympic games, in which he had himself won the chariot race, he had a public announcement made, to the effect that any Greek who thought himself good enough to become Cleisthenes' son-in-law should present himself in Sicyon within sixty days – or sooner if he wished – because he intended, within the year following the sixtieth day, to betroth his daughter to her future husband. Cleisthenes had had a race-track and a wrestling-ring specially made for his purpose, and presently the suitors began to arrive – every man of Greek nationality who had something to be proud of either in his country or in himself. From Sybaris in Italy, then at the height of its prosperity, came Smindyrides the son of Hippocrates, a man noted above all others for delicate and luxurious living, and from Siris, also in Italy, came Damasus the son of Amyris who was nicknamed the Philosopher. Then there was Amphimnestus, the son of Epistrophus, from Epidamnus on the Ionian Gulf, and Males from Aetolia – Males, the brother of Titormus who was the strongest man in Greece and went to live in the remotest part of Aetolia to avoid intercourse with his kind. From the Peloponnese came Leocedes the son of Pheidon, who was ruler of Argos and the man who brought in the system of weights and measures for the Peloponnese – and also turned out the Eleians whose duty it was to manage the Olympic games and proceeded to manage them himself – the wickedest and most arrogant thing ever done by a Greek. Next there was Amiantus, the son of Lycurgus, from Trapezus in Arcadia, and Laphanes, an Azanian from Paeus, whose father Euphorion, the story goes, received Castor and Pollux under his own roof and afterwards kept open house for all comers; and then Onomastus of Elis, the son of Agaeus. From Athens there were two: Megacles, whose father Alcmaeon visited the court of Croesus, and Tisander's son Hippocleides, the wealthiest and best-looking man in Athens. Euboea provided but a single suitor, Lysanias from Eretria, which at that time was at the height of its prosperity; then there was a Thessalian, Diactorides, one of the Scopadae, from Crannon, and, lastly, Alcon from Molossia. This was the list of suitors.

Cleisthenes began by asking each in turn to name his country and parentage; then he kept them in his house for a year, to get to know them well, entering into conversation with them sometimes singly, sometimes all together, and testing each of them for his manly qualities and temper, education and manners. Those who were young he would take to the gymnasia – but the most important test of all was their behaviour at the dinner-table. All this went on throughout their stay in Sicyon, and all the time he entertained them handsomely.

For one reason or another it was the two Athenians who impressed Cleisthenes most favourably, and of the two Tisander's son Hippocleides came to be preferred, not only for his manly virtues but also because he was related some generations back to the family of Cypselus of Corinth.

At last the day came which had been fixed for the betrothal, and Cleisthenes had to declare his choice. He marked the day by the sacrifice of a hundred oxen, and then gave a great banquet, to which not only the suitors but everyone of note in Sicyon was invited. When dinner was over, the suitors began to compete with each other in music and in talking in company. In both these accomplishments it was Hippocleides who proved by far the doughtiest champion, until at last, as more and more wine was drunk, he asked the fluteplayer to play him a tune and began to dance to it. Now it may well be that he danced to his own satisfaction; Cleisthenes, however, who was watching the performance, began to have serious doubts about the whole business. Presently, after a brief pause, Hippocleides sent for a table; the table was brought, and Hippocleides, climbing on to it, danced first some Laconian dances, next some Attic ones, and ended by standing on his head and beating time with his legs in the air. The Laconian and Attic dances were bad enough; but Cleisthenes, though he already loathed the thought of having a son-in-law like that, nevertheless restrained himself and managed to avoid an outburst; but when he saw Hippocleides beating time with his legs, he could bear it no longer. 'Son of Tisander,' he cried, 'you have danced away your marriage.' 'I could hardly care less,' was the cheerful reply. Hence the common saying, 'It's all one to Hippocleides.'

The Tears of Xerxes

Xerxes decided to hold a review of his army. On a rise of ground near by, a throne of white marble had already been specially prepared for his use by the people of Abydos; so the king took his seat upon it and, looking down over the shore, was able to see the whole of his army and navy at a single view. As he watched them he was seized with the desire to witness a rowing-match. The match took place and was won by the Phoenicians of Sidon, to the great delight of Xerxes who was as pleased with the race as with his army. And when he saw the whole Hellespont hidden by ships, and all the beaches and plains of Abydos filled with men, he congratulated himself – and the moment after burst into tears. Artabanus his uncle, the man who in the first instance had spoken his mind so freely in trying to dissuade Xerxes from undertaking the campaign, was by his side; and when he saw how Xerxes wept, he said to him: 'My lord, surely there is a strange contradiction in what you do now and what you did a moment ago. Then you called yourself a lucky man – and now you weep.'

'I was thinking,' Xerxes replied; 'and it came into my mind how pitifully short human life is – for of all these thousands of men not one will be alive in a hundred years' time.'

The Battle of Thermopylae

The Persian army was close to the pass, and the Greeks, suddenly doubting their power to resist, held a conference to consider the advisability of retreat. It was proposed by the Peloponnesians generally that the army should fall back upon the Peloponnese and hold the Isthmus; but when the Phocians and Locrians expressed their indignation at this suggestion, Leonidas gave his voice for staying where they were and sending, at the same time, an appeal for reinforcements to the various states of the confederacy, as their numbers were inadequate to cope with the Persians.

During the conference Xerxes sent a man on horseback to ascertain the strength of the Greek force and to observe what the troops were doing. He had heard before he left Thessaly that a small force was concentrated here, led by the Lacedaemonians under Leonidas of the house of Heracles. The Persian rider approached the camp and took a thorough survey of all he could see – which was not, however, the whole Greek army; for the men on the further side of the wall which, after its reconstruction, was now guarded, were out of sight. He did, none the less, carefully observe the troops who were stationed on the outside of the wall. At that moment these happened to be the Spartans, and some of them were stripped for exercise, while others were combing their hair. The Persian spy watched them in astonishment; nevertheless he made sure of their numbers, and of everything else he needed to know, as accurately as he could, and then rode quietly off. No one attempted to catch him, or took the least notice of him.

Back in his own camp he told Xerxes what he had seen. Xerxes was bewildered; the truth, namely that the Spartans were preparing themselves to die and deal death with all their strength, was beyond his comprehension, and what they were doing seemed to him merely absurd. Accordingly he sent for Demaratus, the son of Ariston, who had come with the army, and questioned him about the spy's report, in the hope of finding out what the behaviour of the Spartans might mean. 'Once before,' Demaratus said, 'when we began our march against Greece, you heard me speak of these men. I told you then how I saw this enterprise would turn out, and you laughed at me. I strive for nothing, my lord, more earnestly than to observe the truth in your presence; so hear me once more. These men have come to fight us for possession of the pass, and for that struggle they are preparing. It is the common practice of the Spartans to pay careful attention to their hair when they are about to risk their lives. But I assure you that if you can defeat these men and the rest of the Spartans who are still at home, there is no other people in the world who will dare to stand firm or lift a hand against you. You have now to deal with the finest kingdom in Greece, and with the bravest men.'

Xerxes, unable to believe what Demaratus said, asked further how it was possible that so small a force could fight with his army. 'My lord,' Demaratus replied, 'treat me as a liar, if what I have foretold does not take place.' But still Xerxes was unconvinced.

For four days Xerxes waited, in constant expectation that the Greeks would make good their escape; then, on the fifth, when still they had made no move and their continued presence seemed mere impudent and reckless folly, he was seized with rage and sent forward the Medes and Cissians with orders to take them alive and bring them into his presence. The Medes charged, and in the struggle which ensued many fell; but others took their places, and in spite of terrible losses refused to be beaten off. They made it plain enough to anyone, and not least to the king himself, that he had in his army many men, indeed, but few soldiers. All day the battle continued; the Medes, after their rough handling, were at length withdrawn and their place was taken by Hydarnes and his picked Persian troops – the King's Immortals – who advanced to the attack in full confidence of bringing the business to a quick and easy end. But, once engaged, they were no more successful than the Medes had been; all went as before, the two armies fighting in a confined space, the Persians using shorter spears than the Greeks and having no advantage from their numbers.

On the Spartan side it was a memorable fight; they were men who understood war pitted against an inexperienced enemy, and among the feints they employed was to turn their backs on a body and pretend to be retreating in confusion, whereupon the enemy would pursue them with a great clatter and roar; but the Spartans, just as the Persians were on them, would wheel and face them and inflict in the new struggle innumerable casualties. The Spartans had their losses too, but not many. At last the Persians, finding that their assaults upon the pass, whether by divisions or by any other way they could think of, were all useless, broke off the engagement and withdrew.

Xerxes was watching the battle from where he sat; and it is said that in the course of the attacks three times, in terror for his army, he leapt to his feet.

Next day the fighting began again, but with no better success for the Persians, who renewed their onslaught in the hope that the Greeks, being so few in number, might be badly enough disabled by wounds to prevent further resistance. But the Greeks never slackened; their troops were ordered in divisions corresponding to the states from which they came, and each division took its turn in the line except the Phocian, which had been posted to guard the track over the mountains. So when the Persians found that things were no better for them than on the previous day, they once more withdrew.

How to deal with the situation Xerxes had no idea; but just then, a man from Malis, Ephialtes, the son of Eurydemus, came, in hope of a rich reward, to tell the king about the track which led over the hills to Thermopylae – and thus he was to prove the death of the Greeks who held the pass.

Later on, Ephialtes, in fear of the Spartans, fled to Thessaly, and in his absence a price was put upon his head by the Amphictyons assembled at Pylae. Some time afterwards he returned to Anticyra, where he was killed by Athenades of Trachis. Athenades killed him not for his treachery but for another reason, which I will explain further on; but the Spartans honoured him none the less on that account. According to another story, it was Onetes, the son of Phanagoras of Carystus, and Corydallus of Anticyra who spoke to Xerxes and showed the Persians the way round by the mountain track. This is entirely unconvincing, my first criterion being the fact that the Amphictyons, presumably after careful inquiry, set a price not upon Onetes and Corydallus but upon Ephialtes of Trachis, and my second, that there is no doubt that the accusation of treachery was the reason for Ephialtes' flight. Certainly Onetes, even though he was not a native of Malis, might have known about the track, if he had spent much time in the neighbourhood – but it was Ephialtes, and no one else, who showed the Persians the way, and I leave his name on record as the guilty one.

Xerxes found Ephialtes' offer most satisfactory. He was delighted with it, and promptly sent off Hydarnes with the troops under his command. They left camp about the time the lamps are lit.

The track was originally discovered by the Malians of the neighbourhood; they afterwards used it to help the Thessalians, taking them over it to attack Phocis at the time when the Phocians were protected from invasion by the wall which they had built across the pass. So long, then, have its sinister uses been known to the Malians! The track begins at the Asopus, the stream which flows through the narrow gorge, and, running along the ridge of the mountain – which, like the track itself, is called Anopaea – ends at Alpenos, the first Locrian settlement as one comes from Malis, near the rock known as Black-Buttocks' Stone and the seats of the Cercopes. Just here is the narrowest part of the pass.

This, then, was the mountain track which the Persians took, after crossing the Asopus. They marched throughout the night, with the mountains of Leta on their right hand and those of Trachis on their left. By early dawn they were at the summit of the ridge, near the spot where the Phocians, as I mentioned before, stood on guard with a thousand men, to watch the track and protect their country. The Phocians had volunteered for this service to Leonidas, the lower road being held as already described.

The ascent of the Persians had been concealed by the oak-woods which cover all these hills, and it was only when they were up that the Phocians became aware of their approach; for there was no wind, and the marching feet made a loud swishing and rustling in the fallen leaves.

Leaping to their feet, the Phocians were in the act of arming themselves when the enemy was upon them. The Persians were surprised at the sight of troops preparing to resist; they had expected no opposition – yet here was a body of men barring their way. Hydarnes asked Ephialtes who they were, for his first uncomfortable thought was that they might be Spartans; but on learning the truth he prepared to engage them. The Persian arrows flew thick and fast, and the Phocians, supposing themselves to be the main object of the attack, hurriedly withdrew to the highest point of the mountain, where they made ready to face destruction. But the Persians with Ephialtes and Hydarnes paid no further attention to them, but passed on along the descending track with all possible speed.

The Greeks at Thermopylae had their first warning of the death that was coming with the dawn from the seer Megistias, who read their doom in the victims of sacrifice; deserters, too, came in during the night with news of the Persian flank movement, and lastly, just as day was breaking, the look-out men came running from the hills. In council of war their opinions were divided, some urging that they must not abandon their post, others the opposite. The result was that the army split: some dispersed, contingents returning to their various cities, while others made ready to stand by Leonidas. It is said that Leonidas himself dismissed them, to spare their lives, but thought it unbecoming for the Spartans under his command to desert the post which they had originally come to guard. I myself am inclined to think that he dismissed them when he realized that they had no heart for the fight and were unwilling to take their share of the danger; at the same time honour forbade that he himself should go. And indeed by remaining at his post he left a great name behind him, and Sparta did not lose her prosperity, as might otherwise have happened; for right at the outset of the war the Spartans had been told by the Delphic oracle that either their city must be laid waste by the foreigner or a Spartan king be killed. The prophecy was in hexameter verse and ran as follows:

Hear your fate, O dwellers in Sparta of the wide spaces;
Either your famed, great town must be sacked by Perseus'
 sons,
Or, if that be not, the whole land of Lacedaemon
Shall mourn the death of a king of the house of Heracles,
For not the strength of lions or of bulls shall hold him,
Strength against strength; for he has the power of Zeus,
And will not be checked till one of these two he has
 consumed.

I believe it was the thought of this oracle, combined with his wish to lay up for the Spartans a treasure of fame in which no other city should share, that made Leonidas dismiss those troops; I do not think that they deserted, or went off without orders, because of a difference of opinion. Moreover, I am strongly supported in this view by the case of the seer Megistias, who was with the army – an Acarnanian, said to be of the clan of Melampus – who foretold the coming doom from his inspection of the sacrificial victims. He quite plainly received orders from Leonidas to quit Thermopylae, to save him from sharing the army's fate. He refused to go, but he sent his only son, who was serving with the forces.

Thus it was that the confederate troops, by Leonidas' orders, abandoned their posts and left the pass, all except the Thespians and the Thebans who remained with the Spartans. The Thebans were detained by Leonidas as hostages very much against their will; but the Thespians of their own accord refused to desert Leonidas and his men, and stayed, and died with them. They were under the command of Demophilus the son of Diadromes.

In the morning Xerxes poured a libation to the rising sun, and then waited till it was well up before he began to move forward. This was according to Ephialtes' instructions, for the way down from the ridge is much shorter and more direct that the long and circuitous ascent. As the Persian army advanced to the assault, the Greeks under Leonidas, knowing that they were going to their deaths, went out into the wider part of the pass much further than they had done before; in the previous days' fighting they had been holding the wall and making sorties from behind it into the narrow neck, but now they fought outside the narrows. Many of the invaders fell; behind them the company commanders plied their whips indiscriminately, driving the men on. Many fell into the sea and were drowned, and still more were trampled to death by their friends. No one could count the number of the dead. The Greeks, who knew that the enemy were on their way round by the mountain track and that death was inevitable, put forth all their strength and fought with fury and desperation. By this time most of their spears were broken, and they were killing Persians with their swords.

In the course of that fight Leonidas fell, having fought most gallantly, and many distinguished Spartans with him – their names I have learned, as those of men who deserve to be remembered; indeed, I have learned the names of all the three hundred. Among the Persians dead, too, were many men of high distinction, including two brothers of Xerxes, Habrocomes and Hyperanthes, sons of Darius by Artanes' daughter Phratagune. Artanes, the son of Hystaspes and grandson of Arsames, was Darius' brother; as Phratagune was his only child, his giving her to Darius was equivalent to giving him his entire estate.

There was a bitter struggle over the body of Leonidas; four times the Greeks drove the enemy off, and at last by their valour rescued it. So it went on, until the troops with Ephialtes were close at hand; and then, when the Greeks knew that they had come, the character of the fighting changed. They withdrew again into the narrow neck of the pass, behind the wall, and took up a position in a single compact body – all except the Thebans – on the little hill at the entrance to the pass, where the stone lion in memory of Leonidas stands today. Here they resisted to the last, with their swords, if they had them, and, if not, with their hands and teeth, until the Persians, coming on from the front over the ruins of the wall and closing in from behind, finally overwhelmed them with missile weapons.

Of all the Spartans and Thespians who fought so valiantly the most signal proof of courage was given by the Spartan Dieneces. It is said that before the battle he was told by a native of Trachis that, when the Persians shot their arrows, there were so many of them that they hid the sun. Dieneces, however, quite unmoved by the thought of the strength of the Persian army, merely remarked: 'This is pleasant news that the stranger from Trachis brings us: if the Persians hide the sun, we shall have our battle in the shade.' He is said to have left on record other sayings, too, of a similar kind, by which he will be remembered. After Dieneces the greatest distinction was won by two Spartan brothers, Alpheus and Maron, the sons of Orsiphantus; and of the Thespians the man to gain the highest glory was a certain Dithyrambus, the son of Harmatides.

The dead were buried where they fell, and with them the men who had been killed before those dismissed by Leonidas left the pass. Over them is this inscription, in honour of the whole force:

> Four thousand here from Pelops' land
> Against three million once did stand.

The Spartans have a special epitaph; it runs:

> Go tell the Spartans, you who read:
> We took their orders, and are dead.

For the seer Megistias there is the following:

> Here lies Megistias, who died
> When the Mede passed Spercheius' tide.
> A prophet; yet he scorned to save
> Himself, but shared the Spartans' grave.

The Battle of Salamis

The Greek commanders at Salamis were at loggerheads. They did not yet know that the enemy ships had blocked their escape at both ends of the channel, but supposed them to occupy the same position as they had seen them in during the day. However, while the dispute was still at its height, Aristides came over in a boat from Aegina. This man, an Athenian and the son of Lysimachus, had been banished from Athens by popular vote, but the more I have learned of his character, the more I have come to believe that he was the best and most honourable man that Athens ever produced. Arrived at Salamis, Aristides went to where the conference was being held and, standing outside, called for Themistocles. Themistocles was no friend of his; indeed he was his most determined enemy; but Aristides was willing, in view of the magnitude of the danger which threatened them, to forget old quarrels in his desire to communicate with him. He was already aware of the anxiety of the Peloponnesian commanders to withdraw to the Isthmus; as soon, therefore, as Themistocles came out of the conference in answer to his call, he said: 'At this moment, more than ever before, you and I should be rivals, to see which of us can do most good to our country. First, let me tell you that the Peloponnesians may talk as much or as little as they please about withdrawing from Salamis – it will make not the least difference. What I tell you, I have seen with my own eyes: they *cannot* now get out of here, however much the Corinthians or Eurybiades himself may wish to do so, because our fleet is surrounded. So go in and tell them that!'

'Good news and good advice,' Themistocles answered; 'what I most wanted has happened – and you bring me the evidence of your own eyes that it is true. It was I who was responsible for this move of the enemy; for as our men would not fight here of their own free will, it was necessary to make them, whether they wanted to do so or not. But take them the good news yourself; if I tell them, they will think I have invented it and will not believe me. Please, then, go in and make the report yourself. If they believe you, well and good; if they do not, it's no odds; for if we are surrounded, as you say we are, escape is no longer possible.'

Aristides accordingly went in and made his report,

saying he had come from Aegina and had been hard put to it to slip through the blockading enemy fleet, as the entire Greek force was surrounded. He advised them, therefore, to prepare at once to repel an attack. That said, he left the conference, whereupon another dispute broke out, because most of the commanders still refused to believe in the report. But while they still doubted, a Tenian warship, commanded by Panaetius, the son of Sosimenes, deserted from the Persians and came in with a full account. For this service the name of the Tenians was afterwards inscribed on the tripod at Delphi among the other states who helped to defeat the invader. With this ship which came over to them at Salamis, and the Lemnian one which previously joined them at Artemisium, the Greek fleet was brought up to the round number of 380. Up till then it had fallen short of that figure by two.

Forced to accept the Tenians' report, the Greeks now at last prepared for action. At dawn the fighting men were assembled and Themistocles was chosen to address them. The whole burden of what he said was a comparison of all that was best and worst in life and fortunes, and an exhortation to the men to choose the better. Then, having rounded off his speech, he gave the order for embarkation. The order was obeyed and, just as the men were going aboard, the ship which had been sent to Aegina to fetch the Sons of Aeacus, rejoined the fleet.

The whole fleet now got under way, and in a moment the Persians were on them. The Greeks checked their way and began to back astern; and they were on the point of running aground when Ameinias of Pallene, in command of an Athenian ship, drove ahead and rammed an enemy vessel. Seeing the two ships foul of one another and locked together, the rest of the Greek fleet hurried to Ameinias' assistance, and the general action began. Such is the Athenian account of how the battle started; the Aeginetans claim that the first to go into action was the ship which fetched the Sons of Aeacus from Aegina. There is also a popular belief that the phantom shape of a woman appeared and, in a voice which could be heard by every man in the fleet, contemptuously cried out: 'Fools, how much further do you propose to go astern?'

The Athenian squadron found itself facing the Phoenicians, who formed the Persian left wing on the western, Eleusis, end of the line; the Lacedaemonians faced the ships of Ionia, which were stationed on the Piraeus, or eastern, end. A few of the Ionians rememberd Themistocles' appeal and deliberately held back in the course of the fighting but most not at all. I could if I wished give a long list of officers in the enemy fleet who captured Greek ships, but the only ones I will mention are Theomester, the son of Androdamas, and Phylacus, the son of Histiaeus, both of them Samians. My reason for naming these two is that Theomestor in reward for this service was invested by the Persians with the lordship of Samos, and Phylacus was enrolled in the catalogue of the King's Benefactors and presented with a large estate. The Persian word for King's Benefactors is *orosangae*.

These two officers, as I say, had some success; but the greater part of the Persian fleet suffered severely in the battle, the Athenians and Aeginetans accounting for a great many of their ships. Since the Greek fleet worked together as a whole, while the Persians had lost formation and were no longer fighting on any plan, that was what was bound to happen. None the less they fought well that day – far better than in the actions off Euboea. Every man of them did his best for fear of Xerxes, feeling that the king's eye was on him.

I cannot give precise details of the part played in this battle by the various Greek or foreign contingents in the Persian fleet; I must, however, mention Artemisia, on account of an exploit which still further increased her reputation with Xerxes. After the Persian fleet had lost all semblance of order, Artemisia was chased by an Athenian trireme. As her ship happened to be closest to the enemy and there were other friendly ships just ahead of her, escape was impossible. In this awkward situation she hit on a plan which turned out greatly to her advantage: with the Athenian close to her tail she drove ahead with all possible speed and rammed one of her friends – a ship of Calynda, with Damasithymus, the Calyndian king, on board. I cannot say if she did this deliberately because of some quarrel she had had with this man while the fleet was in the Hellespont, or if it was just chance that that particular vessel was in her way; but in any case she rammed and sank her, and was lucky enough, as a result, to reap a double benefit. For the captain of the Athenian trireme, on seeing her ram an enemy, naturally supposed that her ship was a Greek one, or else a deserter which was fighting on the Greek side; so he abandoned the chase and turned to attack elsewhere. That, then, was one piece of luck – that she escaped with her life; the other was that, by this very act she raised herself higher than ever in Xerxes' esteem. For the story goes that Xerxes, who was watching the battle, observed the incident, and that one of the bystanders remarked: 'Do you see, my lord, how well Artemisia is fighting? She has sunk an emeny ship.' Xerxes asked if they were sure it was really Artemisia, and was told that there was no doubt whatever – they knew her ensign well, and of course supposed that it was an enemy ship that had been sunk. She was, indeed, lucky in every way – not least in the fact that there were no survivors from the Calyndian ship to accuse her. Xerxes' comment on what was told him is said to have been: 'My men have turned into women, my women into men.'

Among the killed in this struggle was Ariabignes, the son of Darius and Xerxes' brother, and many other well-known men from Persia, Media and the confederate nations. There were also Greek casualties, but not many; for most of the Greeks could swim, and those who lost their ships, provided they were not killed in the actual fighting, swam over to Salamis. Most of the enemy, on the other hand, being unable to swim, were drowned. The greatest destruction took place when the ships which had been first engaged turned tail; for those astern fell foul of them in their attempt to press forward and do some service before the eyes of the king. In the confusion which resulted, some Phoenicians who had lost their ships came to Xerxes and tried to make out that the loss was due to the treachery of the Ionians. But the upshot was that it was they themselves, and not the Ionian captains, who were executed for misbehaviour. While they were speaking, a ship of Samothrace rammed an Athenian; the Athenian was going down, when an Aeginetan vessel bore down upon the Samothracian and sank her, but the Samothracian crew, who were armed with javelins, cleared the deck of the attacking vessel, leapt aboard and captured her. This exploit saved the Ionians; for when Xerxes saw an Ionian ship do such a fine piece of work, he turned to the Phoenicians and, ready as he was in his extreme vexation to find fault with anyone, ordered their heads to be cut off, to stop them from casting cowardly aspersions upon their betters.

Xerxes watched the course of the battle from the base of Mt Aegaleos, across the strait from Salamis; whenever he saw one of his officers behaving with distinction, he would find out his name, and his secretaries wrote it down, together with his city and parentage.

The Persian Ariaramnes, who was a friend of the Ionians and was present during the battle, also had a share in bringing about the punishment of the Phoenicians.

When the Persian rout began and they were trying to get back to Phalerum, the Aeginetan squadron, which was waiting to catch them in the narrows, did memorable service. The enemy was in hopeless confusion; such ships as offered resistance or tried to escape were cut to pieces by the Athenians, while the Aeginetans caught those which attempted to get clear, so that any ship which escaped the one enemy promptly fell among the other. It happened at this stage that Themistocles, chasing an enemy vessel, ran close by the ship which was commanded by Polycritus, the son of Crius, the Aeginetan. Polycritus had just rammed a Sidonian, the very ship which captured the Aeginetan guard-vessel off Sciathus – the one, it will be remembered, which had Pytheas on board, the man the Persians kept with them out of admiration for his gallantry in refusing to surrender in spite of his appalling wounds. When the ship was taken with him and the Persian crew on board, he got safe home to Aegina. When Polycritus noticed the Athenian ship, and recognized the admiral's flag, he shouted to Themistocles and asked him in a tone of ironic reproach if he still thought that the people of Aegina were Persia's friends.

Such of the Persian ships as escaped destruction made their way back to Phalerum and brought up there under the protection of the army.

The most distinguished service at Salamis is admitted to have been that of Aegina; and next after Aegina was

Athens. The greatest individual distinction was won by Polycritus of Aegina, and the two Athenians, Eumenes of Anagyrus and Ameinias of Pallene. It was Ameinias who gave chase to Artemisia, and if he had known that Artemisia was on board, he would never have abandoned the chase until he had either taken her or been taken himself; for the Athenians resented the fact that a woman should appear in arms against them, and the ships' captains had received special orders about her, with the offer of a reward of 10,000 drachmae for anyone who captured her alive. However, as I said, she escaped; some others, too, got away with their ships, and these now lay at Phalerum.

The Athenians have a story that right at the beginning of the action the Corinthian commander Adeimantus got sail on his ship and fled in panic. Seeing the commander making off, the rest of the squadron followed; but when they were off that part of the coast of Salamis where the temple of Athene Sciras stands, they were met by a strange boat. It was all very mysterious, because nobody, apparently, had sent it, and the Corinthians, when it met them, knew nothing of how things were going with the rest of the fleet. From what happened next they were forced to the conclusion that the hand of God was in the matter; for when the boat was close to them, the people on board called out: 'Adeimantus, while you are playing the traitor by running away with your squadron, the prayers of Greece are being answered, and she is victorious over her enemies.' Adeimantus would not believe what they said, so they told him that he might take them with him as hostages, and kill them if the Greeks were not found to have won the battle. On this, he and the rest of the squadron put about, and rejoined the fleet after the action was over. This, as I said, is an Athenian story, and the Corinthians do not admit the truth of it: on the contrary, they believe that their ships played a most distinguished part in the battle – and the rest of Greece gives evidence in their favour.

During the confused struggle a valuable service was performed by the Athenian Aristides, son of Lysimachus, whose high character I remarked upon a little while back. He took a number of the Athenian heavy infantry, who were posted along the coast of Salamis, across to Psyttaleia, where they killed every one of the Persian soldiers who had been landed there.

After the battle the Greeks towed over to Salamis all the disabled vessels which were adrift in the neighbourhood, and then prepared for a renewal of the fight, fully expecting that Xerxes would use his remaining ships to make another attack. Many of the disabled vessels and other wreckage were carried by the westerly wind to a part of the Attic coast called Colias, and in this way it came about that not only the prophecies of Bacis and Musaeus about this battle were fulfilled, but also another prophecy which had been uttered many years previously by an Athenian soothsayer named Lysistratus: the words of this one were, 'The Colian women shall cook their food with oars.' The Greeks had forgotten about it at the time, but it was to happen, all the same, after Xerxes was gone.

A Robe of Many Colours

During his stay at Sardis Xerxes fell in love with Masistes'
wife who was also there. He sent her various messages,
but without success, and at the same time was unwilling
to resort to compulsion out of respect for his brother
Masistes. The woman was well aware of this, and no
doubt her knowledge that Xerxes would not dare to force
her, helped her to hold out against him. Xerxes, therefore,
gave up his other ways of approach, and arranged a
marriage between a daughter of Masistes and this woman
and his own son Darius, under the impression that by this
means he would be more likely to get her. The betrothal
took place with all the usual ceremonies, and Xerxes left
Sardis for Susa. At Susa he received the girl – whose name
was Artaÿnte – into his own house as his son's bride, with
the result that he forgot the mother and transferred his
affections to the daughter – now the wife of Darius. This
time his passion was successful. But as time went on the
connection came to light in the following way: Xerxes'
wife Amestris gave him a long robe, of many colours and

very beautiful, which she had woven with her own hands. Much pleased, he put it on, and, still wearing it, went to visit Artaÿnte – who pleased him no less, with the result that he told her to ask for anything she fancied as a reward for her favours, and he would assuredly grant it. Artaÿnte, who must have been doomed to come to a bad end, together with all her house, asked in reply if the king really meant to give her whatever she demanded, and Xerxes, never suspecting what the request would be, pledged his word to do so. Thereupon she boldly demanded the robe. Xerxes did everything he could think of to get out of giving it, simply because he was afraid of Amestris, who already guessed what was going on and would now, he feared, find her suspicions confirmed. He offered her cities, gold in unlimited quantity, an army – a thoroughly Persian gift – under her sole command; but all in vain – nothing would do but the robe. So he gave it her, and she, in great delight, put it on, and gloried in wearing it.

When Amestris found out, as she soon did, that Artaÿnte had the robe, it was not against her that her anger was directed. On the contrary, she thought that the girl's mother, Misistes' wife, was the person responsible for the whole trouble, and consequently plotted her destruction.

She waited for the day when her husband the king gave his Royal Supper – a ceremony which occurs once a year, on the king's birthday. The Persian word for the supper is *tycta*, a word equivalent, in our language, to *perfect*; it is the one occasion in the year when the king anoints his head and gives presents to the Persians. Then, when the day for the supper came, she asked Xerxes for her present – Masistes' wife. Xerxes, who understood the reason for her request, was horrified, not only at the thought of handing over his brother's wife, but also because he knew she was innocent. But Amestris persisted – and, moreover, the law of the Supper demanded that no one, on that day, might be refused his request; so at last, much against his will, Xerxes was forced to consent. Then, having told his wife to do with the woman what she pleased, he sent for his brother. 'Masistes,' he said, 'you are my brother and Darius' son; in addition to that, you are a good man. Do not live any longer with your present wife – I will give you my own daughter instead. Marry her: part with your present wife – I do not approve of your keeping her.'

'My lord,' replied Masistes in astonishment, 'this is indeed a strange proposal! What is the use in your telling me to get rid of a wife who is the mother of grown-up sons and daughters – one of whom you married to your own son – and who is, moreover, everything I could wish for, and to marry your daughter instead? No, sire; I will do neither of these things, proud though I am that you should think me worthy of your daughter. Do not, I beg, force this request upon me; but let me live with my wife in peace. You will find another man as good as I am for your daughter.'

Xerxes was angry at this reply. 'Very well, then,' he cried, 'I will tell you, Masistes, what you have done for yourself: I no longer offer you the chance of marrying my daughter – nor will you live another day with that wife of yours. Thus may you learn to accept a proffered gift.'

'Master,' said Masistes, 'you have not killed me yet!' And without another word he left the room.

Meantime, while Xerxes was talking to his brother, Amestris sent for the soldiers of the royal bodyguard and had Masistes' wife horribly mutilated. Her breasts, nose, ears, and lips were cut off and thrown to the dogs; then her tongue was torn out and, in this dreadful condition, she was sent home. Masistes, who knew as yet nothing of what had happened, but suspected mischief of some sort, hurried to his house; and when he saw his wife's fearful injuries, at once he took counsel with his sons and with them and certain other friends set off for Bactria, with the intention of stirring up revolt in the province and of so doing serious harm to the king. He would, I think, undoubtedly have succeeded had he had time to reach the Bactrians and Sacae; for he was greatly beloved by both, and was, moreover, governor of Bactria. But Xerxes discovered his purpose and sent an armed force in pursuit, which caught him on the road and killed him together with his sons and all the men under his command. So ends the story of Xerxes' love and the death of Masistes.